WOULD YOU RATHER?

GAME BOOK FOR KIDS!

Thank you for your purchase!

We hope you enjoy this book! If you have any questions, feedback, or notice any printing issues, please feel free to reach out to us at serenagladwellpublishing@gmail.com

We'd love to hear from you!

Got a moment to spare? Your feedback is incredibly valuable and helps us continue creating great books. Head over to our books on Amazon and leave a review or rating!

Of course, if you have any enquiries, questions or just want to reach out, then you are very welcome to contact us at serenagladwellpublishing@gmail.com

Chapters

Introduction

Would You Rather? Game Book for Kids! is designed to spark laughter, creativity, and meaningful conversations for your family and friends. It's packed with hundreds of fun, silly, and thought-provoking questions that are perfect for road trips, family game nights, or even just a few giggles at the dinner table.

Here's what makes this book special:

- Family-Friendly Fun: Every question is crafted with kids in mind, ensuring all content is age-appropriate and safe for young imaginations.
- Encourages Creativity: These playful scenarios inspire kids to think outside the box, express themselves, and explore their imaginations.
- Builds Connections: Sharing answers and reasoning behind choices is a great way to learn more about each other, deepen family bonds, and make lasting memories.

Whether your child is a jokester, a thinker, or has a big imagination, this book offers something for everyone. There's no need for extra materials or complicated rules—just open to a page, start reading, and let the fun begin!

So, gather everyone around and enjoy the silly debates, surprising answers, and endless giggles as you play together. We hope this book brings as much joy to your family as it brought us while creating it!

Happy playing! 😊

Serena Gladwell

Game Rules

Have fun answering a variety of silly, funny, and thought-provoking "Would You Rather?" questions with your friends and family. There's no right or wrong answer—just laughter, creativity, and maybe a few tough decisions!

How To Play:

- **Gather Players:**
  - You can play alone, with a friend, or with a group of players. The more, the merrier!
  - For two or more players, take turns to read out the questions, starting with the oldest in the group. After a question, pass the book to the person to the right of you.
- **Choose a Question:**
  - Read the questions in chronological order, or pick a random question from whichever topic from the book, and read the question aloud to the group.
- **Decide Your Answer:**
  - Think carefully: which option would you choose and why?
  - Each player takes turns sharing their choice. It's not required but you can add to the fun by explaining why you chose your answer, or encouraging other to give explanations to their answers! Feel free to get as silly or as serious as you like.
- **Keep score (optional):**
  - If you like playing competitively, you can add voting after everyone answers, the group can vote on the funniest, most creative, or most unexpected answer and assign that person a point. Set the number of questions in the game. The one with the most points is the winner!

Tips for Fun:

- Be Honest! The fun comes from hearing what people really think. Who knows, maybe you learn something new about the people you are playing with, and they can learn something new about you!
- Be Respectful. Everyone has different preferences—there are no wrong answers!
- Get Creative. Use your imagination to come up with hilarious explanations.

Winning the Game:

There's no official winner in "Would You Rather?"—the goal is to laugh, have fun, and enjoy the silly scenarios together! If you would like to get competitive, keep score as described on the previous page!

Let the fun begin! 🎉

Food & Drink

Welcome to the Food & Drink chapter, where things are about to get deliciously weird!

Get ready to face some of the silliest, yummiest, and toughest food scenarios you've ever imagined. From your favorite snacks to out-of-this-world flavors, this chapter will challenge your taste buds and test your imagination.

You'll laugh, you'll cringe, and you might even get a little hungry along the way! So grab a snack (because you'll probably want one!) and dive into this mouth-watering adventure.

Would you rather

eat only pizza for a month

OR

only pasta for a month?

Would you rather

have your favorite cereal for dinner

OR

your favorite pizza for breakfast?

Would you rather

eat a giant lollipop

OR

a giant marshmallow?

Would you rather

have a meat feast pizza

OR

have a four-cheese pizza?

Would you rather

eat ice cream in the arctic

OR

eat hot soup in the desert?

Would you rather

eat only vegetables for a week

OR

only fruits for a week?

Would you rather

have a chocolate-filled donut with chocolate icing and sprinkles

OR

a triple chocolate cookie with a molten chocolate center

Would you rather

only be able to eat green foods

OR

only orange foods?

Would you rather

eat spicy salsa on everything

OR

sweet syrup on everything?

Would you rather

eat a sandwich with pickles

OR

a salad with peanut butter?

Would you rather

never have any chicken again

OR

never have any beef or pork again?

Would you rather

eat a lime

OR

eat a whole jalapeno?

Would you rather

give up Italian food for a month

OR

give up Mexican food for a month

Would you rather

drink a glass of tomato juice

OR

drink a glass of grapefruit juice?

Would you rather

have gummy worms on your sandwich

OR

sprinkles on your pizza?

Would you rather

have only crunchy food forever

OR

only soft food forever?

Would you rather

eat a bowl of cereal with orange juice instead of milk

OR

eat tomato soup with Nutella mixed in?

Would you rather

eat an entire jar of pickles

OR

a whole bag of lemons?

Would you rather

have a small portion of your favorite meal

OR

unlimited portions from a buffet that only serves salad?

Would you rather

have a cake with ketchup frosting

OR

a hot dog with chocolate sauce?

Would you rather

eat a pizza with pineapple

OR

a peanut butter and jelly pizza?

Would you rather

eat an ice cream with mayonnaise

OR

fries with chocolate sauce?

Would you rather

only eat foods that start with the

letter "P"

OR

"M"?

Would you rather

eat a popsicle that tastes like

broccoli

OR

ice cream that tastes like spinach?

Would you rather

never eat cheese

OR

never eat bread?

Would you rather

never eat another pizza

OR

never eat another burger?

Would you rather

only ever have water for a drink

OR

only have fruit and veg for snacks

Would you rather

eat a raw onion

OR

eat a raw Brussel sprout?

Would you rather

never have ketchup again

OR

never have mayo again?

Would you rather

give up chips for a year

OR

give up chocolate for a year?

— Would you rather —

never have smoothies again

OR

never have milkshakes again?

— Would you rather —

only be able to eat dessert forever

OR

never eat dessert again?

— Would you rather —

unlimited cola for a month

OR

unlimited chocolate milk for a month?

Would you rather

have to eat a tablespoon of wasabi

OR

a tablespoon of cinnamon powder?

Would you rather

eat food that is very spicy for a

month

OR

eat food that is bland for a month?

Would you rather

a bowl full of nachos

OR

a bowl full of french fries?

Would you rather

have unlimited food at McDonald's

OR

have unlimited food at KFC

Would you rather

make your absolute favorite snack
healthy

OR

make vegetables more tasty

Would you rather

live without food beginning with a C

OR

live without food beginning with a B?

Adventure & Travel

Pack your bags and buckle up—this chapter is taking you on the adventure of a lifetime!

Whether you're climbing mountains, exploring jungles, or flying to faraway planets, the Adventure & Travel chapter is full of thrilling choices that will spark your imagination and test your courage.

So, grab your map, put on your explorer hat, and get ready to choose your next epic journey. Where will **YOU** go next?

Would you rather

discover a real dinosaur fossil

OR

find a rare animal in the wild?

Would you rather

stay in a castle for a night

OR

an underwater hotel?

Would you rather

visit a real-life Jurassic Park

OR

explore Hogwarts?

Would you rather

try jet skiing on the ocean

OR

ride a snowmobile through the

arctic?

Would you rather

visit outer space

OR

explore the deep sea?

Would you rather

go to a safari park

OR

a theme park?

23

Would you rather

experience an erupting volcano

OR

experience a tornado?

Would you rather

sled with huskies in the snow

OR

ride a camel across a desert?

Would you rather

have unlimited free travel but only

to one country

OR

get to go anywhere in the world

once in 5 years for free?

Would you rather

only visit beach destinations

OR

only mountain destinations for the rest of your life?

Would you rather

stay in an all-inclusive resort and never leave

OR

have to camp and explore every day?

Would you rather

explore an underwater coral reef

OR

explore a cave system?

Would you rather

visit Disneyland

OR

a real-life dinosaur museum?

Would you rather

ride a dragon

OR

be friends with a talking animal?

Would you rather

explore an abandoned castle

OR

explore a ghost town?

Would you rather

live like an explorer on a deserted island

OR

like a ranger in a huge national park?

Would you rather

go stargazing on a mountaintop

OR

see bioluminescent plankton on a beach?

Would you rather

visit the pyramids in Egypt

OR

the Great Wall of China?

Would you rather

visit a city with tall skyscrapers

OR

a small town with cozy cottages?

Would you rather

go skiing in the mountains

OR

surfing in the ocean?

Would you rather

sleep in an igloo

OR

in a jungle treehouse?

Would you rather

visit the Eiffel Tower in Paris

OR

Statue of Liberty in New York?

Would you rather

take a road trip in an RV

OR

sail across the ocean on a boat?

Would you rather

visit a city with lots of history

OR

a modern, futuristic city?

Would You Rather? Game Book For Kids

Would you rather

be able to teleport anywhere in the world

OR

time-travel to any historical event?

Would you rather

have unlimited access to any amusement park

OR

have unlimited access to any cinema

Would you rather

have a backpack that can carry everything and weigh nothing

OR

a magic camera that takes pictures of memories in your mind

30

Would you rather

scuba diving with sharks

OR

snorkeling with jellyfish?

Would you rather

survive a zombie apocalypse for a
night with your friends

OR

find your way out an escape room
with your friends?

Would you rather

have a zip line in your backyard

OR

a rock-climbing wall?

Would you rather

camp overnight in the jungle

OR

in the desert?

Would you rather

skydive from a plane

OR

bungee jump off a cliff?

Would you rather

ride the fastest roller coaster

OR

go on the tallest water slide?

Funny, Silly & Weird

Welcome to the wackiest part of the book, where normal rules don't apply! This chapter is packed with the funniest, silliest, and downright weirdest Would You Rather? questions you've ever seen.

From talking animals to the silliest superpowers, these scenarios will make you laugh out loud and scratch your head at the same time. So, loosen up, let your imagination go wild, and get ready to dive into the absurd. How silly can YOU get?

Would you rather

have a pet dragon

OR

have a pet unicorn?

Would you rather

have to wear itchy clothes

OR

wet socks all day?

Would you rather

spaghetti hair that grows when

you're hungry

OR

popcorn that pops out of your ears

when you're excited?

Funny, Silly & Weird

Would you rather

step on a LEGO

OR

hit your funny bone?

Would you rather

always have a runny nose

OR

always be on the verge of a sneeze?

Would you rather

walk around with a pebble in your

shoe

OR

with an itchy tag on your shirt?

35

Would you rather

have an elephant-sized hamster

OR

a hamster-sized elephant?

Would you rather

only be able to whisper

OR

only be able to shout?

Would you rather

have a rewind button

OR

a fast-forward button for your day?

Would you rather

have hair that changes color with

your mood

OR

shoes that make silly sounds?

Would you rather

shoot webs like Spiderman

OR

fly like Superman?

Would you rather

have uncontrollable farts forever

OR

have a squeaky voice forever?

37

Would you rather

have an extra eye

OR

have an extra ear?

Would you rather

only be able to walk backward

OR

only be able to crawl?

Would you rather

have super sticky fingers

OR

super stretchy arms?

Would you rather

have a magical backpack that can

hold anything

OR

shoes that let you walk on walls?

Would you rather

walk around all day with ketchup on

your shirt

OR

walk around all day with toilet paper

stuck to your shoe?

Would you rather

have to hop everywhere you go

OR

have to tiptoe everywhere you go?

Would you rather

smell like stinky cheese

OR

always have garlic breath?

Would you rather

talk like a robot

OR

walk like a penguin?

Would you rather

have a face that changes colors with

your mood

OR

a laugh that sounds like a donkey?

Would you rather

talk in rhymes all the time

OR

sing everything you say?

Would you rather

hiccup every time you speak

OR

yawn every time someone talks to you?

Would you rather

have rainbow-colored teeth

OR

glow-in-the-dark hair?

Would you rather

sound like a duck when you laugh

OR

bark like a dog when you sneeze?

Would you rather

have an extra-long nose like

Pinocchio

OR

big, floppy ears like an elephant?

Would you rather

be as tiny as an ant

OR

as big as a giant for one day?

42

Would you rather

have the power to control fire

OR

control water?

Would you rather

have to wear a tutu for a day

OR

a superhero cape for a day?

Would you rather

have toes that are as long as your fingers

OR

fingers as short as your toes?

Would you rather

always have to hop like a frog

OR

slither like a snake to get around?

Would you rather

be a giant butterfly

OR

a tiny dinosaur?

Would you rather

burn your tongue

OR

have brain freeze?

Funny, Silly & Weird

Would you rather

be able to only whisper

OR

only shout for the rest of your life?

Would you rather

always have to wear shoes that are
too big

OR

wear clothes that are too small?

Would you rather

always have an itch you can't scratch

OR

a sneeze you can't get out?

45

Animals & Pets

Get ready to unleash your wild side in the Animals & Pets chapter! 🐾 Whether you love fluffy kittens, giant dinosaurs, or magical creatures, this is the place where all your favorite animals come to life—with some hilarious twists!

Will you choose to have a talking parrot follow you, have the camouflage of a chameleon, or eat lunch with a monkey? These questions are packed with fun, fur, and a little bit of imagination.

So, grab your leash, saddle, or magic wand, and let's explore the wild and wonderful world of animals!

Would you rather

be able to jump like a kangaroo

OR

swing through trees like a monkey?

Would you rather

spend a day hanging out with

penguins in Antarctica

OR

koalas in Australia?

Would you rather

discover a worm in your apple

OR

discover a snake in your toilet?

47

Would you rather

be as strong as a gorilla

OR

as fast as a cheetah?

Would you rather

be able to camouflage like a

chameleon

OR

be able to regenerate body parts

like a starfish?

Would you rather

be able to talk to animals

OR

turn into any animal you choose?

48

Would you rather

have claws like a bear

OR

sharp teeth like a shark?

Would you rather

have 5 dogs

OR

have 5 cats as pets?

Would you rather

be able to live underwater as a shark

OR

soar high in the sky as an eagle?

49

Would you rather

spend a day speaking with parrots

OR

spend a day eating bananas with monkeys?

Would you rather

be able to dig like a mole

OR

climb like a mountain goat?

Would you rather

be a brave lion

OR

an intelligent dolphin

50

Would you rather

hold a snake for a minute

OR

hold a tarantula for a minute?

Would you rather

have a tiger as a pet

OR

have a monkey as a pet?

Would you rather

pick up a porcupine

OR

get stung by a wasp?

51

Would you rather

have an aquarium at home

OR

have farm animals in the garden?

Would you rather

have a pet hamster that loves to run

on a wheel

OR

a pet bird that sings all day?

Would you rather

cuddle with a fluffy bunny

OR

a soft kitten?

Would you rather

have a pet turtle that moves slowly

OR

a pet rabbit that hops everywhere?

Would you rather

have a pet that pees everywhere

OR

have a pet that tears up everything?

Would you rather

go diving in a shark cage and see the

most dangerous sharks

OR

a go on a open roof Jeep ride

through the Serengeti

53

Would you rather

sleep in a room with lots of spiders

OR

sleep in a room with a rooster that

is constantly crowing?

Would you rather

be a giant whale in the ocean

OR

a tiny hummingbird in the forest?

Would you rather

chased by a swarm of bees

OR

chased by angry swans?

Would you rather

have a hungry mosquito follow you everywhere

OR

a fly land on your food every time you eat?

Would you rather

ride on a giant tortoise across the sea

OR

ride on a speedy ostrich across the savanna?

Would you rather

have an elephant as a pet

OR

have an owl as a pet?

Tough Choices

Welcome to the Tough Choices chapter—the ultimate test of your decision-making skills! These questions aren't just fun—they're tricky, challenging, and guaranteed to make you think twice (or three times!).

Would you rather face your greatest fear or give up your favorite treat forever? The choices might be tough, but the laughs and surprises will make it all worth it.

Are you ready to tackle some of the most difficult decisions ever? Take a deep breath, stay strong, and dive in. What will YOU choose when the going gets tough?

Would you rather

be the best at one skill

OR

really good at a lot of things?

Would you rather

live without TV

OR

live without video games?

Would you rather

have your parents read all your text messages ever

OR

have your parents spy on you all day for a month?

Would you rather

lose your ability to read

OR

lose your ability to write?

Would you rather

be famous for something silly

OR

unknown but amazing at something

important?

Would you rather

only watch movies forever

OR

only listen to music forever?

Would you rather

have no internet for a month

OR

no snacks for a month?

Would you rather

always feel a little too hot

OR

a little too cold?

Would you rather

fast forward 5 years

OR

rewind 5 years

Would you rather

have no pets

OR

have five pets you have to care for

all by yourself?

Would you rather

always have to wear your least

favorite color

OR

only eat your least favorite

vegetable?

Would you rather

have only indoor activities

OR

only outdoor activities for fun?

Would you rather

have a job where you work with animals

OR

have a job where you go to outer space?

Would you rather

have $1 million dollars

OR

have 1 million friends?

Would you rather

live on a farm with lots of animals

OR

live in a big city with lots of places to visit?

61

Would you rather

live 100 years in the past

OR

100 years in the future?

Would you rather

get paid to do what you love doing

OR

win the lottery?

Would you rather

always be 10 minutes late

OR

always be 20 minutes early?

Would you rather

tell the truth and lose a friend

OR

tell a lie to keep the friendship?

Would you rather

never get embarrassed

OR

never feel scared?

Would you rather

never watch a comedy movie again

OR

never watch an action movie again?

Would you rather

have to wake up super early every

day

OR

have to sleep early every night?

Would you rather

always have to do extra chores

OR

never get an allowance?

Would you rather

be the captain of a ship

OR

be the pilot of an aircraft?

Would you rather

have only one best friend

OR

lots of friends who aren't close?

Would you rather

experience life in Ancient Egypt

OR

experience life in the dinosaur era?

Would you rather

live in a tiny house with your family

OR

a big house all alone?

Would you rather

forget your favorite memory

OR

never be able to make new ones?

Would you rather

always stand out in a crowd

OR

always blend in?

Would you rather

never be allowed to draw again

OR

never be allowed to write stories again?

Would you rather

be the oldest kid in your family

OR

the youngest kid in your family?

Would you rather

always get blamed for things you didn't do

OR

never get credit for things you did do?

Would you rather

always have to eat super healthy food

OR

always have to exercise a lot?

67

Would you rather

lose your ability to laugh

OR

lose your ability to cry?

Would you rather

find something you have lost

OR

receive some brand new?

Would you rather

eradicate all crime on Earth

OR

eradicate all illnesses on Earth?

Would you rather

never go on a family vacation again

OR

never have birthday parties again?

Would you rather

always have to tell the truth

OR

always have to keep secrets?

Would you rather

always be the first one to try

something new

OR

always wait until others try it first?

Would you rather

be able to change one thing about yourself

OR

one thing about the world?

Would you rather

always know what people think about you

OR

never know?

Would you rather

lose the ability to see colors

OR

lose the ability to taste your favorite food?

Would you rather

have to redo every mistake you

make

OR

never get to try again?

Would you rather

be super busy every day

OR

have nothing to do all the time?

Would you rather

always have to do what you're told

OR

always have to figure things out on

your own?

Would you rather

always know the answer to every question

OR

always be able to make people laugh?

Would you rather

get locked out of your house

OR

locked in your room?

Would you rather

have a family movie night every week

OR

a family game night every week?

Would you rather

spend a whole day helping your

parents clean the house

OR

helping them with yard work?

Would you rather

have a job as a zookeeper

OR

as a video game designer?

Would you rather

become a doctor

OR

become a lawyer?

Would you rather

be a movie star

OR

a professional athlete?

Would you rather

have a magic wand that grants wishes

OR

a book that tells the future?

Would you rather

have VIP seats at sports games

OR

have VIP seats at movie premieres?

Would you rather

lose your favorite toy

OR

never be able to buy a new one?

Would you rather

be the funniest comedian

OR

the best magician?

Would you rather

never celebrate your birthday again

OR

never celebrate a holiday again?

That's Gross!

Welcome to the Gross Chapter, where things get totally yucky and hilariously icky! 🤢 If you love squishy, slimy, stinky, or downright disgusting scenarios, this is the place for you.

Would you rather eat a spider-flavored ice cream or swim in a pool of jelly? These questions are guaranteed to make you cringe, laugh, and maybe even squirm a little. But don't worry—it's all in good fun!

So, get ready to face the grossest, weirdest, and funniest challenges ever. How much ickiness can YOU handle?

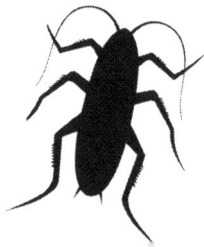

That's Gross!

Would you rather

swim in a pool of slime

OR

swim in a pool of mud?

Would you rather

pick your own nose and eat your

booger

OR

pick your ear and eat the earwax?

Would you rather

find a bug in your ice cream

OR

find a rat in your lunchbox?

Would you rather

stroke a slimy frog

OR

hold wiggly worms?

Would you rather

smell a dirty diaper

OR

two year expired milk?

Would you rather

step in something squishy barefoot

OR

accidentally sit on something sticky?

That's Gross!

Would you rather

poop in a dirty public toilet

OR

poop in the bushes without toilet paper?

Would you rather

sneeze into a tissue that someone else has sneezed into

OR

chew on a pencil someone else chewed?

Would you rather

have to brush your teeth with soap

OR

have to wash your hair with vinegar?

79

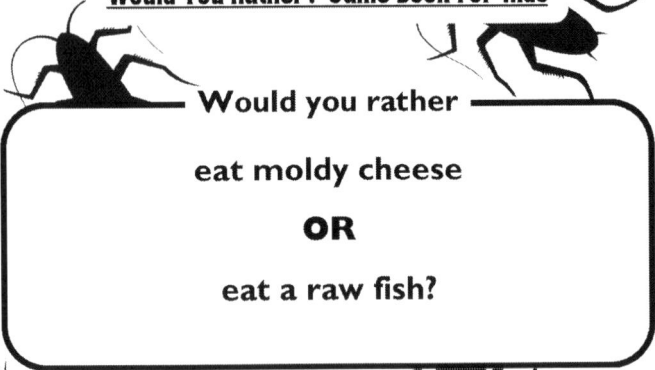

Would you rather

eat moldy cheese

OR

eat a raw fish?

Would you rather

pee yourself in public

OR

walk in public without pants for an

hour?

Would you rather

have a pet that drools all the time

OR

have a pet that sheds all the time?

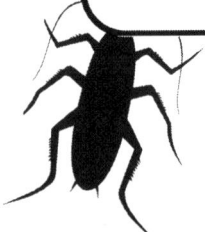

That's Gross!

Would you rather

have smelly feet

OR

itchy armpits?

Would you rather

shower once a month

OR

sweat everytime you go outside?

Would you rather

eat a plate of spaghetti with worms

in it

OR

a sandwich with a live bug inside?

81

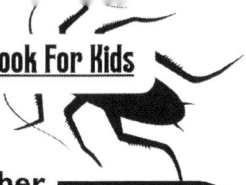

—— **Would you rather** ——

not brush your teeth for a month

OR

not wash your hair for a month?

—— **Would you rather** ——

step in dog poop barefoot

OR

have bird poop land on your head?

—— **Would you rather** ——

have a snail crawl across your face

OR

a bug crawling in your hair?

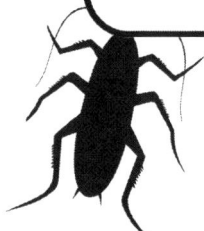

Would you rather

drink water from a fish tank

OR

eat food found in a dumpster?

Would you rather

not shower for a month

OR

not change your clothes for a month?

Would you rather

eat two week expired bread

OR

drink two week expired milk

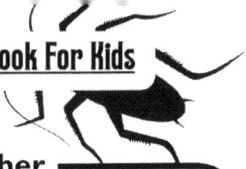

Would you rather

have to lick the bottom of your shoe

OR

a dirty kitchen counter?

Would you rather

have a constant bad smell under

your nose

OR

a bad taste in your mouth?

Would you rather

have boogies in your ear

OR

have earwax in your nose?

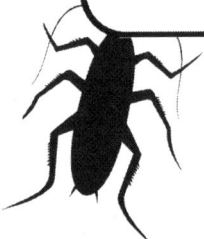

84

Would you rather

eat a spoonful of dog food

OR

eat a spoonful of cat food?

Would you rather

sit in a bathtub full of worms

OR

sit in a bathtub full of sewage?

Would you rather

have to smell a stinky garbage can

for a day

OR

eat something from it?

Would you rather

accidentally drink from a stranger's

water bottle

OR

eat leftover sandwich crust from a

stranger's lunchbox

Would you rather

chew gum that has been stuck

underneath a table

OR

eat a burger on the floor that has

been stepped on?

Would you rather

be covered in honey

OR

be covered in mustard?

Would you rather

eat a cold spaghetti sandwich

OR

a warm ketchup smoothie?

Would you rather

smell like a skunk for a week

OR

have an itchy nose for a month?

Would you rather

pick up a napkin someone has

sneezed into

OR

pick up a napkin someone has wiped

their sweat on?

School

Welcome to the School Chapter, where your classroom adventures take a fun and wacky turn!

Whether you love school, hate it, or just wish recess lasted all day, this chapter is packed with silly, tricky, and hilarious school-related scenarios that will make you laugh, think, and maybe even wish your school days were this exciting!

So, grab your backpack, sharpen your pencils, and get ready to choose your way through the wildest school experiences ever. What will YOU choose?

Would you rather

miss the bus

OR

forget your homework at home?

Would you rather

accidentally call your teacher 'mom'?

OR

accidentally call your crush 'mom'?

Would you rather

have a teacher who always calls on you for answers to questions

OR

have a teacher who never allows talking in class?

Would you rather

forget to bring your gym shoes

OR

forget to bring your homework to

school?

Would you rather

be chosen last for a team

OR

not be chosen at all?

Would you rather

be the principal for a day

OR

get to choose the school lunch for a

month?

Would you rather

help a friend with their homework

and not finish yours

OR

not help them and get a good grade?

Would you rather

always have to share your lunch

OR

never get to sit with your friends?

Would you rather

have a large house party with a lot

of kids you don't know

OR

have a small gathering with only

your closest friends?

Would you rather

be the only new kid in your school

OR

be older than everyone in your class

by two years?

Would you rather

be the class clown

OR

the teacher's pet?

Would you rather

have school all year but only four

days a week

OR

six days a week for eight months of

the year?

Would you rather

have school start two hours earlier

OR

end two hours later?

Would you rather

write a long essay

OR

solve 100 math problems?

Would you rather

share your desk with someone

messy

OR

someone who never talks?

Would you rather

have gym class every day

OR

have music class every day?

Would you rather

never have math as a subject again

OR

never have english as a subject again?

Would you rather

use a really blunt pencil

OR

use a pen that always smudges?

Would you rather

be the first to present in class

OR

be the last to present in class?

Would you rather

never have field trips

OR

never have another gym lesson
again?

Would you rather

let someone at school cut in line

OR

argue and make a scene to keep
your spot?

Would you rather

play dodgeball every recess

OR

play tag every recess?

Would you rather

have a substitute teacher every day

OR

have the same teacher all year?

Would you rather

do a surprise show-and-tell every

day

OR

a pop quiz every week?

School

Would you rather

drop your lunch tray in the cafeteria

OR

trip and fall in front of your class?

Would you rather

have to give a big speech at school

with no preparation

OR

sing a song in front of the whole

school?

Would you rather

have your backpack break at school

OR

forget your lunch at home?

Would you rather

join a club with all your friends but not enjoy it

OR

a club you love without your friends?

Would you rather

always be the one to organize group activities

OR

always just go along with what others plan?

Would you rather

have to team up with someone who never listens

OR

someone who never helps?

Would you rather

eat school lunch every day

OR

have to pack your own lunch every day?

Would you rather

always have to sit at the front of the class

OR

always have to sit away from friends?

Would you rather

have no summer vacation

OR

no winter and easter holiday break?

99

Would you rather

have a boring teacher who never gives homework

OR

a fun teacher who gives a lot of homework?

Would you rather

have parents evening every month

OR

have tests on every subject every month?

Would you rather

have a snow day

OR

go to a school disco?

Would you rather

make a new friend every day

OR

keep the same group of friends

forever?

Would you rather

have a friend who always tells jokes

OR

one who is very clever?

Would you rather

only see your friends at school

OR

only see them outside of school?

Would you rather

accidentally wave at someone who

wasn't waving at you

OR

accidentally talk to someone who

wasn't listening?

Would you rather

wear a shirt thats two sizes too big

OR

wear a shirt thats two sizes too

small?

Would you rather

have to tell a funny joke that no one

laughs at

OR

try to sing a song and forget the

words?

School

Would you rather

be locked inside your school for a week

OR

be locked inside your house for a week?

Would you rather

have to go to school on weekends

OR

do homework every night?

Would you rather

have to move to a new school every year

OR

never have summer vacation?

Creepy & Spooky

Welcome to the Creepy and Spooky Chapter, where the choices are mysterious, a little scary, and a whole lot of fun! From haunted houses to eerie forests, this chapter is full of chills, thrills, and spine-tingling decisions.

Would you rather spend the night in a creepy castle or face a ghost in your closet?

So, turn down the lights, summon your courage, and get ready to dive into the spooky side of "Would You Rather?" What will YOU choose in the face of fright?

Would you rather

spend the night in a haunted house

OR

spend the night in a spooky forest?

Would you rather

find a monster under your bed

OR

find a monster hiding in your closet?

Would you rather

hear creepy whispers in the dark

OR

see glowing eyes in the dark?

105

Would you rather

walk through a graveyard at midnight

OR

explore an abandoned castle at midnight?

Would you rather

have a bat flying around your room

OR

a spider crawling on your bed?

Would you rather

have to eat a cursed apple with a worm inside

OR

have to drink a witches' potion from her cauldron?

106

Would you rather

hear giggling coming from another room when you're home alone?

OR

footsteps upstairs when you're home alone?

Would you rather

have to wear skeleton gloves forever

OR

have to wear vampire fangs forever?

Would you rather

meet Dracula

OR

meet Frankenstein?

107

Would you rather

have to sleep in a coffin

OR

have to sleep on a bed of cobwebs?

Would you rather

hear creepy music in the

background

OR

see eerie shadows everywhere you

go?

Would you rather

be a ghost who can float

OR

a witch who can fly?

Would you rather

have to live in a world of zombies

OR

have to live in a world of vampires?

Would you rather

dress up as a goblin for a day

OR

dress up as a witch for a day

Would you rather

go trick-or-treating in a spooky city

neighborhood

OR

go trick-or-treating in an eerie quiet

village neighborhood?

Would you rather

encounter a creepy clown when

walking in the dark

OR

encounter a demon with fangs when

walking in the dark?

Would you rather

explore a haunted shipwreck

OR

an abandoned mansion?

Would you rather

wear a pumpkin on your head all

day

OR

have sticky, slimy hands for a week?

Would you rather

eat a bowl of wriggling spaghetti

OR

drink glowing green punch?

Would you rather

wear an eye-patch for a week

OR

a cobweb hat for a day?

Would you rather

visit a haunted house with floating furniture

OR

visit a haunted house with walls that talk?

Would you rather

make friends with a friendly ghost

OR

make friends with a talking black cat

Would you rather

explore a creepy attic

OR

explore a spooky basement?

Would you rather

find a doll that moves on its own

OR

a teddy bear that talks at night?

Would you rather

be locked in a spooky library overnight

OR

be locked in a spooky museum overnight?

Would you rather

have a light that flickers on and off

OR

have a floor that creaks when stepped on?

Would you rather

find a secret passageway behind a bookshelf

OR

find a hidden trapdoor underneath the carpet?

— Would you rather

find maggots in your food

OR

find black, hairy spiders in your

bedroom?

Would you rather

be lost in a pumpkin patch

OR

be lost in a corn maze?

Would you rather

eat eyeball and tongue soup

OR

eat brain and gut stew?

Would you rather

have an eye that keeps popping out

OR

have a head that keeps slumping

over?

Would you rather

be a mad scientist

OR

be a wizard?

Would you rather

be stuck in an elevator for an hour

OR

be stuck on a ferris wheel for an

hour?

— Would you rather —

be chased by a mummy

OR

be chased by a swarm of crows?

— Would you rather —

touch something slimy in the dark

OR

step on something squishy in the dark?

— Would you rather —

hear a knock at your window in the middle of the night?

OR

scratching at your door in the middle of the night?

Science & Technology

Welcome to the Science & Technology Chapter, where the future is in your hands! From high-tech gadgets to visiting the outer reaches of space, this chapter is full of mind-blowing questions that will take you to the cutting edge of imagination.

Make choices over video games, gadgets, outer space, sci-fi and much more! Would you rather have a hoverboard or a jetpack?

Time for you to dive into a world of innovation and adventure!

Would you rather

have a robot friend

OR

a virtual reality gaming room?

Would you rather

be the first to land on Mars

OR

be the first to live on the Moon?

Would you rather

discover more about dinosaurs

OR

discover more about outer space?

118

Would you rather

be a character in a video game

OR

be a character in a cartoon?

Would you rather

have super strength

OR

have super speed?

Would you rather

have your own jetpack

OR

have your own flying car?

Would you rather

never use TikTok again

OR

never use YouTube again?

Would you rather

only play multiplayer games

OR

only play single-player games

forever?

Would you rather

have a microscope that can see

atoms

OR

a telescope that can see other

galaxies?

Would you rather

have a time machine

OR

have a teleporter?

Would you rather

live in a virtual world for a day

OR

control a robot in real life for a day?

Would you rather

have the ability to freeze time

OR

speed it up?

Would you rather

have shoes that let you jump super

high

OR

shoes that run super fast?

Would you rather

only use a tablet for the rest of your

life

OR

only use a smartphone for the rest

of your life?

Would you rather

have the ability to fly

OR

have the ability to turn invisible?

Would you rather

find out if there are aliens are out there

OR

discover how the universe was formed?

Would you rather

have glasses that let you see far away

OR

ones that let you see in the dark?

Would you rather

visit a black hole

OR

travel to the edge of the universe?

Would you rather

have a 3D printer that can make

almost anything (not a drone)

OR

have a remote-controlled drone

that can fly around the world?

Would you rather

defy gravity

OR

defy time?

Would you rather

make your favorite video game feel

more like real life

OR

live a day inside your favorite game?

Would you rather

live in a space station

OR

live in an underwater city?

Would you rather

meet a friendly alien

OR

meet a friendly robot?

Would you rather

have a holographic pet

OR

have a robotic helper pet?

Would you rather

have super-fast Wi-Fi everywhere

OR

unlimited battery life on all your devices?

Would you rather

have a huge comic book collection

OR

a huge video game collection?

Would you rather

discover a new species and name them

OR

discover a new planet and name it?

Holidays & Celebrations

Welcome to the Holidays & Celebrations Chapter, where every day feels like a party! ❄ From birthday surprises to festive traditions, this chapter is packed with fun-filled questions about all your favorite holidays and special occasions.

Would you rather have a snowball fight at Christmas or a water balloon fight at your birthday party?

Get ready to get into celebratory vibes and choose your way through the happiest and most festive moments ever!

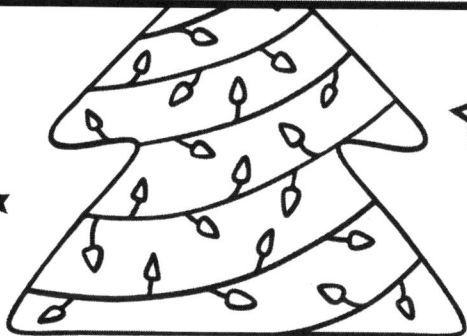

Would you rather

have lots of presents on your birthday

OR

go on a vacation on your birthday?

Would you rather

carve pumpkins

OR

paint Easter eggs?

Would you rather

have a magic show at your party

OR

a puppet show at your party?

Would you rather

play musical chairs at a party?

OR

play pin the tail on the donkey at a party?

Would you rather

have a snowball fight at your party

OR

a water balloon fight at your party?

Would you rather

sing karaoke at a party

OR

dance in a dance-off at a party?

Would you rather

receive one giant present

OR

receive ten small presents?

Would you rather

have a pool party

OR

have a sleepover party?

Would you rather

have a bouncy castle

OR

have a giant slide at your party?

Would you rather

have your birthday on a school day

OR

have christmas as a school day?

Would you rather

decorate a Christmas tree

OR

build a snowman?

Would you rather

wear a Santa hat all day

OR

wear reindeer antlers all day?

Would you rather

live in a gingerbread house

OR

a snowy igloo?

Would you rather

have a Christmas tree that smells

like cookies

OR

have a Christmas tree that smells

like peppermint?

Would you rather

have lights that blink on your tree

OR

multi-color lights on your tree?

Would you rather

wear a red nose like Rudolph

OR

wear pointy ears like an elf?

Would you rather

have more turkey at Christmas

OR

have more Christmas pudding at

Christmas

Would you rather

get an extra present

OR

get an extra dessert?

Would you rather

go sledding on Christmas Day?

OR

ice skating on Christmas Day?

Would you rather

have a Christmas dinner with Santa

OR

a snowball fight with elves?

Would you rather

have no Christmas presents

OR

no Christmas tree?

Would you rather

eat only candy canes for a whole week

OR

only gingerbread cookies for a whole week?

Would you rather

eat a giant chocolate bunny

OR

eat a giant candy cane?

Would you rather

sing Christmas carols to strangers

OR

wear a funny Christmas outfit all day?

135

Would you rather

decorate the biggest Christmas tree

in the world

OR

make the most gingerbread houses

ever?

Would you rather

only watch Christmas movies for a

whole year

OR

listen to Christmas music for a

whole year?

Would you rather

ride with Santa on his sleigh

OR

chill with Santa at his North Pole

workshop?

Would you rather

never celebrate Christmas again

OR

celebrate it every month?

Would you rather

meet Frosty the Snowman

OR

meet Rudolph the Red-Nosed

Reindeer?

Would you rather

wear sunglasses outside on

Christmas

OR

wear a sun hat outside on

Christmas?

Would you rather

have Easter be in winter

OR

Christmas be in spring?

Would you rather

have your birthday in the winter

OR

have your birthday in the summer?

Would you rather

celebrate Easter without chocolate

OR

celebrate Easter without the easter

egg hunt?

Would you rather

wear a silly costume for every

holiday

OR

dress super fancy?

Would you rather

only celebrate holidays with food

OR

only celebrate holidays with games?

Would you rather

have a birthday party at a fun place

but only for an hour

OR

at home but for the whole day?

Would you rather

have your birthday party at a zoo

OR

have your birthday party at an

amusement park?

Would you rather

skip your birthday one year to

double it the next year

OR

celebrate it twice in one year?

Would you rather

have a cake that tastes amazing but

looks bad

OR

one that looks amazing but doesn't

taste good?

Manufactured by Amazon.ca
Bolton, ON